Table of Contents

Chapter 1: Ghana

Ghana

Ghana is literally at the center of the world. Ghana holds one of the largest oil reserves discovered this century, only to be rivaled by an oil reserve found in Guyana in 2022. Ghana is rich in resources like gold cobalt, ore, gold, and oil. Ghana has abundant food resources and the capabilities and conditions to grow even more amounts of food for biofuel, cosmetics, and other industrial processes need development.

Food exports will need to be processed, cataloged, and shipped to people all around the world. Ghana has positioned itself to be the next global Powerhouse like China or Japan; which in the last century became leaders in manufacturing and global supply chain. On top of being a safe place to live and raise children, Ghana could be an ideal location for young and aging Africans worldwide.

Ghana has one flaw, and that is its currency. The Ghana Cedi fluctuates as the world changes from day to day. This leaves Ghana's citizens confused, often cash-strapped, and wondering why their people are still suffering when it has so many resources to offer the world. Building a country from the ground up takes time, 1957 was only 66 years ago. It will take variety in the private sector to start creating jobs and developing career paths. Ghana is where the opportunity needs to be leveraged.

The year of return was an introduction for diasporans to Ghana into all that Ghana has to offer by way of development, investment and leisure. In this short book, we will discuss why global Africans in the diaspora are intrigued by Ghana. We will also look at some of Ghana's hidden gems.

Some of you may be considering a move to Ghana and if that's the case, we want you to join our **Facebook group:** Moving to Ghana Q&A. In this group, you can find even more detailed information about making your transition to Ghana and doing that successfully. Topics are cataloged by hashtag. If you want to know where a good meet-up spot is, search in the group **#meetup** and find previous posts, information about hundreds of Ghana-specific topics, posts, and discussions on a range of topics. We get private messages and calls every day from global Africans who think they are going to pack up their lives in the west and move to Ghana on a whim. We have to talk them down from this high and give them a dose of reality:

"You cannot pick up and move to Ghana, you need to visit first!"

Join our Facebook Group!

Of course, you can always reach out to us for concierge, tailored travel itineraries, and questions. To visit our office, please call ahead.

Abusa Travels Offices

✉ **Address: 25 Boundary Rd, East Legon**

📞 **Emails: Info@abusuatravels.com**

Phone: +233 30 255 1221 (Ghana)
Website: abusuatravels.com
Whatsapp: +233 26 620 6006
Facebook: @AbusuaTravels
FB Groups: Moving to Ghana: Q&A
Instagram: @AbusuaTravels

For this publication, we want to strictly discuss traveling and visiting Ghana to get to know the place; before transitioning into becoming an ex-pat in Africa. Moving to a new country is extremely nuanced and expensive for the average westerner. Making a move to Africa will take months but most likely years of preparation and planning with trusted guides and assistance from people on the ground.

Who is this book written for?

This book was written for curious people. Those people who are adventurous, and who want to do their research before they embark on a life-changing experience through travel. This book is for people who are thinking about traveling to Ghana, West Africa; for the first time. This book is for people who may have never traveled internationally, and want to get an honest and solid opinion about when, where, why, and how to come to Ghana and feel fulfilled with their choice.

Ghana is not for the weak-hearted; Africa is not for the weak! You may find that some conveniences that you experience in the West are available but not the same. It's kind of like when you order Chinese food from a new place, that's not *"your place"*, and it just tastes different. There's nothing wrong with it; it just tastes different and that's the type of mentality you need to travel abroad.

There are three main rules to travel:

1. **If you are going to need it, bring it with you!**
2. Traveler's diarrhea **does** exist
3. You must come to Ghana and have the best time of your life.

Most global Africans go back to Africa to have a cathartic or spiritual experience or connection. Whether you practice Ife or Christianity you will find what you are looking for in Ghana. The best thing about Africa in general and Ghana specifically, is that everything you are looking for is right there. It might not be within Uber's delivery range but if you are looking for it in Ghana you will find it, which includes love as well but I digress.

Ghana collected its independence on March 6, 1957. Since its break from the colonial strongholds Ghana has been struggling to stabilize its economy, feed its citizens, and provide jobs and housing for the masses. Due to the *"African president syndrome"* where corruption overshadows good policy; local Ghanaians suffer imaginable poverty due to the mismanagement of funds. Ghana has seen droughts, floods, and has had periods of feast and famine since its independence. Today we are embarking on a new time and new period for Ghana in which they are at the top of the minds of global Africans. Global Africans want to find a connection with where they come from.

Young and aging Africans in the global diaspora are suffering and crying out for a remedy to the hundreds of years of subjugation and disregard from their own country's leaders. Africa is not perfect. Ghana is not perfect. There is much to learn and much to change to accommodate the vast amount of global Africans who want to return home.

Ghana does have all of the amenities that we are used to, it's the convenience that we are used to that we have to build up. For us to live the lives that we are used to in the west we will have to come to Ghana and invest, develop businesses and the digital infrastructure to create jobs, create housing and use the skills that we have developed in the west to help improve Ghana.

We need to make keeping it comfortable for those who live there now, a priority, while we simultaneously focus on those of us who want to move to Ghana in the future. Ghana is ripe and it's ready. It's ready for investment, it's ready and open for travel; it's ready for us to come and permeate through the streets and attend festivals and fill up its churches. Ghana needs us to buy its newly manufactured cars and build sustainable houses, and for us to live in those houses permanently.

Ghana is ready for us to come and create jobs for the people already there To teach them new skills and to help them upscale and become involved in the global market as it moves forward. As we embark on Web 2.0 (that is how you found this book, perhaps through Google Search) only 50 % of Africans have access to the internet, according to BBC. While 49% of Ghanaians live in poverty according to (DW news.

Although we have the statistics in our own country that mirror these numbers we're seeing in Ghana we need to make a conscious decision on where we will focus our energy and our time to help build and strengthen our Global black community.

Black Lives Matter

Since the murder of George Floyd, there has been a global focus on black and blackness. The protests in the Summer of 2020 went on for weeks. The brutality that black men suffer at the hands of American and European law enforcement was the focal point of the protesting and rallying that happened that year. Due to divine intervention, everyone was at home using the internet sitting in front of screens right where we needed them to be to see that black lives do matter.

Ghana has positioned itself to accept the throng of global African people who were ready to come back to Africa, wanting to live and to make their lives. The year of Return happened in 2019 into 2020, it was a year-long celebration many of us missed a boat; we were unaware of. Droves of celebrities attended events, festivals, and parties in December 2019, which has now been coined, *"Dutty December"* in Ghana.

With that same energy, we are building this pathway for you to join us and explore Ghana but most importantly by coming back to Africa if only to visit. we can't expect that every global African has the means or the interest to move back to Africa but we can reach out and help those who are looking for assistance and guidance in making the visit or the transition in peace.

What we are doing here is assisting you in making some tough decisions. Vacationing in Ghana is not an everyday experience, we want to be sure that you get the most out of your time.

We want to make sure that you are:

1. Achieving personal goals,
2. Fully experiencing your homeland,,
3. diving into traditional and cultural Foods,
4. Letting the air, water, and land cheer you up of your pent-up frustration.

We want you to feel less and less of that as you get closer and closer to your goal of exploring Africa but most important, going to Ghana to find peace.

Who we are:

Abusua Travels was the brainchild of Nana Michael in 2019. While he was on deployment in Afghanistan as a contractor for the US Government Mike realized that something was brewing, there was a lot of focus on his home country of Ghana. He had always dreamed of creating a business that would allow him to mingle and meet different people.

In early 2020 Mike made the leap, he quit his job and formed Abusua Travels with the hope that he could help increase awareness of Africa and assist his global brothers and sisters while they come back and visit their Motherland. During his course of returning home, the world fell into Pandemic lockdown and Mike was stuck in Dubai in his hotel room for 14 weeks until quarantine lifted. At that time online traffic was moving at a swift pace Mike linked up with a marketing partner and the rest has been history.

Abusua Travels came to life on the internet and in the hearts of the early outliers looking to connect with Ghana in late 2019 and early 2020. Almost instantly we were flooded with questions about how to come to Ghana and how people from all over the world messaged and called asking how to make a transition to living in Ghana. With that much traffic, we decided to create a Facebook group to help people sort through some of their questions and to get acclimated to the Ghanaian way of life.

It has been a labor of love Abusua Travels staff has cultivated some memorable experiences on the ground for a little under 5 years now! We have grown the group to nearly 6,000 members and we are just getting started.

From all-inclusive touring to providing group accommodations Abusua Travels is your go-to tour guide and all-around Travel Agency for planning all things Ghana. Our clientele is the best, everyone we encounter has been warm and ready to explore Ghana with all the gloves off.

We have been able to take people from all over the world hiking and sailing. They have experienced healing through cleansing baths and naming ceremonies. We have whatever it is you are looking for when you come to Ghana. We humbly ask that you choose Abusua Travels for all of your travel needs when coming to Ghana. You will find that we are trustworthy and efficient as you make your plans and travel with us. Be sure to check the reviews in this book and all of our reviews on Google.

Why we wrote this book:
An introduction to Ghana

"Going to Ghana" started trending in 2017-18 at the onset of the Year of Return, a marketing initiative that began in West Africa and spread Like wildfire. Set up as a means to get Global Africans to return to the continent to spend their money but most importantly to bring their knowledge and help in areas of Economic Development across the continent of Africa.

The initiative was slow going not due to the lack of marketing but due to the lack of Interest from Global Africans about Africa. The year of return is a 50-year initiative started in West Africa to enlighten the global diaspora about the challenges and opportunities that exist in Africa and specifically Ghana. As Africa steps into its place as the next Global hotspot Ghana quickly became a leader in the push for diasporan attention.

Ghana was successful in implementing a marketing campaign that sprawled not only North America but across Europe and inspired young Global Africans to return to Africa to explore and find their roots. We are invited to eat good food, stay in the world's best accommodations and explore the world's best beaches. With an implied expectation that we invest our time, and money as well as expertise to bring Africa into its rightful place as the world's next powerful continent.

Africa is made up of 54 distinct countries with their amalgamation of cultures, dialects, dress, music and so much more. This publication is going to focus on Ghana and all of its beauty and what it has to share with the global African diaspora.

Abusua Travels Reviews:

 **De Ri**
6 reviews

⋮

★ ★ ★ ★ ★ 5 months ago

Used Abusua Travel and Tour services for an airport pick up for myself and my family and it was perfect. The vehicle was very clean and spacious with enough room for our 8 pieces of luggage. The drivers were very courteous, professional and helpful with all our luggage. Would definitely use again and recommend for others coming to Ghana! 10/10.

 **Amber M**
7 reviews

⋮

★ ★ ★ ★ ★ a year ago

I had an absolutely amazing trip to Ghana thanks to Abusua Travel and Tour Services! I am a solo female traveler, and this was my first trip to Africa. Abusua Travels handed everything for me from air bnb recommendations to securing my visa on arrival to bringing me to different sites throughout the country. My guide Michael made sure that I saw all of the sites on our itinerary. He was available throughout the trip if I needed anything. My trip would not have been the stress-free, beautiful experience that it was had I not booked with Abusua Travel and Tour Services!! Highly recommend!

S Shanikqua Woodard
4 reviews

 2 months ago

I have nothing but great things to say about Abusua Travels & Tour Services. Micheal and his staff went beyond our expectations! We stayed an hour out of the city, and AbusuaTravels still accommodated us. Michael always made himself available to my family and I. He even called us while we were in the States prepping to come to Ghana. He made sure that we had all of our documentation for our journey. He provided a phone for us, so that we wouldn't have to buy a sims card. He even took us grocery shopping twice since we were staying away from the city. To add icing on the cake, I asked Michael if he could help me get a surprise birthday cake for My Aunt's birthday. Not only did he come through for me, but even offered to pickup the cake for me. My aunt was so happy!!! What tour company do you know that would provide all of these perks? The entire experience felt authentic! Micheal and his team treated us like their family. I would highly recommend AbusuaTravels. My family and I will definitely call on AbusuaTravels when we come back to Ghana GH

L Libby Down
Local Guide · 57 reviews

 11 months ago

Michael was amazing. From the first message I sent him to the final goodbye he was fantastic. The itinary was jam packed and my guests really left feeling they had a seen a wide variety of Ghana!

Dana Freeman
6 reviews

⋮

★ ★ ★ ★ ★ 2 months ago

Mike and his team are phenomenal. This was NOT a cookie cutter tour! He catered to our every need. Mike was there from the beginning until the end. He is hilarious and very personable. We were always taken care of. The entire experience was seamless. I wish I could have stayed longer, however I will be back to take additional tours with Mike and his team. Mike is awesome. I would give Abusua travel 20 stars if I could.

Aqua Safari Experience

Abusua Travels

Package Inclusive

- Transportation
- Buffet | Water| Snacks
- Horse ride | Jet-ski ride
- Swimming | Fish feeding
- Crocodile Island | Boat cruise
- Hot air balloon
- Entrances fees
- Professional guide

$200 Pre person

www.abusuatravels.com

Book Now
0266206006

ACCRA TOUR
$70.00

CAPE COAST TOUR
$190.82

KWAHU TOUR
$400.00

About Us

We organize tours for individuals, groups and families ranging from cultural, historical, adventure and wildlife safari.

Contact for More Info

📞 +233 266 206006
📍 GA-390-1278
✉ info@abusuatravels.com
🌐 www.abusuatravels.com

Package Inclusions

- Tours
- Entrance fees
- Snacks
- Meals
- Water / Soft Drinks
- Transportation
- Wifi
- Tour Guide
- Hotel Pickup & Drop off

For our special customer, no terms and conditions

📌🐦f📷@abusuatravels

Chapter 2: Planning your trip

Traveling abroad is an amazing experience that can open up an entirely new world of possibilities. Lean in and start exploring new cultures and environments, try new foods, and make new friends, the world is your oyster when you travel.

Traveling gives you the opportunity to gain a better understanding of the people around you. You begin to gain a deeper appreciation for other cultures and ways of life. You gain a greater understanding of yourself and your own values and beliefs in relation to the world around you. Traveling abroad is a great way to learn more about your own capabilities.

When you travel, you push yourself out of your comfort zone and try new things. You explore new cities and countries and experience a different way of life. This will help you gain the confidence and self-awareness to make the most out of your own life.

Traveling abroad is a great way to make business connections as well. By meeting people from different countries and cultures, you learn to create bonds that can last a lifetime. Traveling abroad can be an amazing way to relax and take a break from your daily life. Whether you travel solo or with friends and family, it's a wonderful opportunity to escape your routine and recharge.

Explore new destinations, try new foods, and participate in unique experiences that you might not be able to find at home. Traveling abroad can provide an opportunity for personal growth and self-discovery.

When you are away from your familiar surroundings and routines, you have the chance to reflect on your life and consider what is most important to you. You may even come back from your travels with a new perspective and a renewed sense of purpose.

However, traveling abroad can also present challenges and obstacles like language barriers or cultural differences that can be difficult to navigate. But these challenges can also be a learning opportunity, as they can help you develop flexibility, adaptability, and resilience.

By embracing the unexpected and stepping out of your comfort zone, you can grow and develop as a person.

Traveling abroad can be a wonderful experience that is sure to enrich your life in countless ways. Whether you are seeking adventure, relaxation, or personal growth, traveling abroad can provide the perfect opportunity to explore the world, make new connections, and discover new parts of yourself. So, pack your bags, grab your passport, and get ready to embark on the journey of a lifetime!

Discovering the Beauty of Ghana

Ghana is the land of vibrant culture, stunning beaches, and fascinating wildlife! No matter what activities you choose to do here, you're guaranteed to have a wonderful experience. Whether you're an adventurer, a beach-goer, or a culture enthusiast, this country has something for everyone.

Let's start with exploring the culture. Ghana has a rich history and a diverse cultural heritage that is reflected in its festivals, music, dance, and cuisine. The people of Ghana are friendly, warm, and always ready to welcome visitors.

Take a visit to the National Museum in Accra, where you can learn about the history of Ghana and the cultures of its 16 regions and various ethnic groups. There are over 50 indigenous languages in Ghana. Ghana has some languages spoken by the majority of the people including Akan, Ewe, Ga, Dagaare, and Dagbani as well as English which is the official language of the country.

If you prefer to immerse yourself in the local culture, attend one of the many festivals that take place throughout the year. The Homowo Festival in the Ga-Dangme people, the Akwasidae Festival in the Ashanti Kingdom, and the Odwira Festival in the Akuapem people are just a few examples of the dazzling cultural events you can witness while in Ghana.

Let's head to the beaches. Ghana boasts some of the most beautiful and pristine beaches in Africa. Find a quiet spot to relax and soak up the sun or an action-packed day filled with water sports, Ghana has something for everyone. Labadi Beach in Accra is one of the most popular spots for both locals and tourists alike. If you're looking for a more secluded spot, head
to Kokrobite Beach, which is known for its stunning sunsets and clear waters.

Exploring Ghana's National Parks

Kakum National Park is located in the central region of Ghana and covers an area of 375 square kilometers. The park is renowned for its stunning canopy walkway, which is the highlight of many visitors' trips to the park. The walkway is suspended 35 meters above the ground and provides breathtaking views of the surrounding rainforest. The park is also home to a rich and diverse array of wildlife, including monkeys, birds, and insects, making it a great destination for nature lovers.

In addition to the canopy walkway, Kakum National Park also offers several other attractions, including the Kakum Nature Trail, which is a 2.5-kilometer trail that takes visitors through the heart of the park's lush rainforest. The park is also home to several birdwatching spots, making it a great destination for bird enthusiasts.

Mole National Park is located in the Northern region of Ghana and is one of the largest national parks in the country. It covers an area of 4,840 square kilometers and is home to a wide variety of wildlife, including elephants, antelopes, baboons, and warthogs. Visitors to the park can take guided walks or go on a wildlife drive to see the animals in their natural habitat.

Discover the wildlife! Mole National Park is also known for its stunning landscapes, including rolling hills, savannah plains, and rocky outcrops. Visitors can also take a guided hike to the top of Mole Hill, which provides panoramic views of the surrounding landscape. The park is also home to several lodges, making it a great destination for those who want to spend multiple days exploring the park and its surrounding areas.

The Assin Manso Ancestral River Site, located in the Central Region of Ghana, is a sacred and historically significant site that holds cultural and spiritual significance for the people of the Ashanti Kingdom. The site is known for being the location where enslaved Africans were washed and purified before being sent to the Americas and the Caribbean. The river, which runs through the site, is believed to have healing properties, making it a place of pilgrimage for many people of the Ashanti Kingdom.

The history of the Assin Manso Ancestral River Site dates back to the early 17th century when the trans-Atlantic slave trade was at its peak. Before being sent to the Americas and the Caribbean,enslaved Africans were taken to the Assin Manso Ancestral River Site to be washed and purified.

This was done in a ritual known as the "African Dunking Ceremony," which was believed to cleanse the slaves of their past lives and prepare them for their new lives in bondage. The ritual was performed by the elders of the Ashanti Kingdom and was considered a sacred tradition.

Today, the Assin Manso Ancestral River Site is a popular tourist destination and a place of pilgrimage for people from all over the world who are interested in learning about the history of the trans-Atlantic slave trade and the culture of the Ashanti Kingdom. The site has been restored and preserved, and visitors can now witness the African Dunking Ceremony and learn about the history of the site.

Many come to visit for the waters historical significance, the Assin Manso Ancestral River Site is also known for its natural beauty. The river is surrounded by lush tropical vegetation and is home to a variety of plant and animal species. Visitors can also witness traditional Ashanti cultural practices, such as drumming and dancing, which are performed in honor of the ancestors who were taken from the site and sold into slavery.

The Assin Manso Ancestral River Site is a unique and important cultural and spiritual site that holds great significance for the people of the Ashanti Kingdom and for those interested in the history of the trans-Atlantic slave trade. Whether you are interested in learning about the history of slavery or simply want to experience the natural beauty of the site, the Assin Manso Ancestral River Site is a must-visit destination for anyone traveling to the Central Region of Ghana.

**Bonus Packing List

- ☐ Passport and visa (if required)
- ☐ COVID-19 documentation
- ☐ Cash and credit/debit cards (must declare any amount over $9,000 to customs)
- ☐ Travel insurance documents
- ☐ Mosquito repellent (incense, lotions & Sprays)
- ☐ Sunscreen
- ☐ Water bottle with a filter
- ☐ First aid kit
- ☐ Portable charger for electronic devices
- ☐ Adaptor for electrical outlets
- ☐ Travel-sized toiletries(toothbrush, toothpaste, shampoo, over-the-counter meds like allergy pills, antacids, etc.)
- ☐ Lightweight, comfortable clothing
- ☐ Long sleeve shirts and long pants
- ☐ Shoes suitable for hiking or walking
- ☐ Umbrella or rain jacket
- ☐ Warm clothing for cooler weather
- ☐ Hat and sunglasses
- ☐ Travel towel
- ☐ Portable water purification tablets or UV sterilizers
- ☐ Portable flashlight or headlamp
- ☐ This guidebook
- ☐ Cameras or other recording devices
- ☐ Journal or notebook for keeping memories
- ☐ Reusable shopping bag
- ☐ Cash in small denominations for tipping and small purchases
- ☐ Relevant clothing for visits to religious or cultural sites.

Non-perishable food items that travel well

- ☐ Dried Fruits
- ☐ Nuts
- ☐ Jerky
- ☐ Granola Bars
- ☐ Protein Bars
- ☐ Energy Bars
- ☐ Dehydrated snacks
- ☐ Trail Mix
- ☐ Crackers/Biscuits
- ☐ Dried Soup
- ☐ Canned Fish
- ☐ Freeze Dried Meals
- ☐ Chips/Crisps
- ☐
- ☐
- ☐

NOTES:

_____

_____

_____

_____

_____

_____

_____

_____

_____

Chapter 3: The Wonders of Traveling Abroad

Traveling abroad is a fantastic way to broaden your horizons and experience new and exciting things. Whether it's a short trip or a long vacation, traveling can be a transformative experience that allows you to gain a new perspective on the world.

One of the biggest benefits of traveling abroad is the opportunity to immerse yourself in different cultures. You can try new foods, learn about local customs, and experience different ways of life. This can be a great way to gain a deeper understanding and appreciation for other cultures, which can help to break down cultural barriers and promote understanding.

Another benefit of traveling abroad is the opportunity to make new friends and connections. By meeting people in different countries and cultures, you can learn more about them and create bonds that can last a lifetime. This can be especially true if you stay with a local host or participate in cultural activities, such as language classes or cultural tours.

Traveling can also be a great way to relax and take a break from your daily life. Whether you're exploring new cities, relaxing on a beach, or engaging in outdoor activities, traveling can provide a much-needed respite from the stresses of everyday life.

By disconnecting from your normal routine and surrounding yourself with new sights and sounds, you can return home feeling refreshed and rejuvenated. Traveling abroad can also be a great way to improve your mental and physical health. Studies have shown that traveling can have a positive impact on mental well-being, reducing symptoms of depression and anxiety and improving overall happiness levels. Traveling can also be a great way to be physically active, whether it's exploring new destinations on foot, participating in outdoor activities, or simply experiencing a new way of life.

Traveling abroad is a fantastic way to learn new things and develop new skills. Whether you're taking a cooking class, learning a new language, or trying new activities, traveling can provide you with a unique opportunity to learn and grow. So why not start planning your next adventure today?

The Assin Manso Ancestral River Site

The Assin Manso Ancestral River Site, located in the Central Region of Ghana, is a sacred and historically significant site that holds great cultural and spiritual significance for the people of the Ashanti Kingdom. The river, which runs through the site, is believed to have healing properties, making it a place of pilgrimage for many people of the Ashanti Kingdom.

The history of the Assin Manso Ancestral River Site dates back to the early 17th century when the trans-Atlantic slave trade was at its peak.

Today, the Assin Manso Ancestral River Site is a popular tourist destination and a place of pilgrimage for people from all over the world who are interested in learning about the history of the trans-Atlantic enslavement trade and the culture of the Ashanti Kingdom. The site has been restored and preserved, and visitors can now witness the African Dunking Ceremony and learn about the history of the site.

In addition to its historical significance, the Assin Manso Ancestral River Site is also known for its natural beauty. The river is surrounded by lush tropical vegetation and is home to a variety of plant and animal species. Visitors can also witness traditional Ashanti cultural practices, such as drumming and dancing, which are performed in honor of the ancestors who were taken from the site and sold into slavery.

The Assin Manso Ancestral River Site is a unique and important cultural and spiritual site that holds great significance for the people of the Ashanti Kingdom and for those interested in the history of the trans-Atlantic slave trade. Whether you are interested in learning about the history of enslavement or simply want to experience the natural beauty of the site, the Assin Manso Ancestral River Site is a must-visit destination for anyone traveling to the Central Region of Ghana.

Ghana's festivals

African festivals are renowned for their rich cultural heritage and dashing colors. From the intricate patterns and designs of traditional outfits to the bright hues that adorn every aspect of these celebrations, the costumes worn during African festivals are a feast for the eyes.

One of the most iconic African festival costumes is the Kente cloth of Ghana. The Kente cloth is a brightly colored, hand-woven material that is often worn in the form of a robe or sash during important cultural celebrations. The cloth features intricate patterns and designs, each of which carries a unique cultural significance. From the diamond-shaped motifs that symbolize wisdom and creativity to the zigzag patterns that symbolize the ups and downs of life, every aspect of the Kente cloth is imbued with meaning.

Another popular African festival costume is the Dashiki, a brightly colored, loose-fitting tunic that is widely worn throughout the continent. The Dashiki is often decorated with bold geometric patterns and is paired with coordinating pants or skirts to create a complete ensemble. The style and design of the Dashiki vary depending on the region, with some versions featuring elaborate embroidery or beadwork, while others are more simple and understated.

Outside of traditional robes and tunics, many African festivals also feature costumes that incorporate intricate headwear, body adornments, and accessories. From the beaded headbands and necklaces of the Zulu people to the elaborate face painting and body scarification of the Maasai, these cultural costumes serve as a visual representation of a person's heritage and identity.

African festival costumes are a vivid expression of the continent's rich cultural heritage, featuring a diverse range of styles, designs, and colors that reflect the unique identities and traditions of various African tribes. Whether you're witnessing a festival in person or simply admiring these beautiful costumes from afar, they are sure to leave a lasting impression and inspire a deeper appreciation for the African culture.

The Rich History of Ghanaian Kente Cloth

Kente cloth is a brightly colored, handwoven cloth that has become synonymous with Ghanaian culture and heritage. For centuries, it has been an important part of the country's history and has been worn by royalty, common people, and special occasions. In this chapter, we will explore the rich history of Kente cloth and its significance in Ghanaian culture.

Kente cloth is believed to have originated from the Ashanti kingdom in the 17th century. It was initially worn by Ashanti royalty as a symbol of their high status and wealth. The cloth was made from indigenous materials and was woven on hand-operated looms. Over time, it evolved into a symbol of cultural pride and was worn by people of all classes and ethnic groups.

Kente cloth is known for its bright, bold colors and intricate patterns. Each color and pattern holds significant cultural and historical meaning. For example, the yellow color symbolizes richness and wealth, while the red color represents the blood of those who died in battles to protect their kingdom. The patterns themselves often depict proverbs, legends, and historical events, making Kente cloth a visual representation of Ghana's rich cultural heritage.

Kente cloth has played a large role in political activism. During the anti-colonial movement in the 20th century, many Ghanaians wore Kente cloth as a symbol of their solidarity and resistance against colonial rule. In modern times, Kente cloth is still worn on special occasions, such as weddings and funerals, and is often used as a symbol of national pride.

Kente cloth is still handwoven today, using the same techniques that have been passed down for generations. Each cloth is unique and can take several weeks to several months to weave, depending on its complexity. The cloth is made from cotton or silk and is woven on a loom using a process known as strip weaving. The strips are then sewn together to form the finished cloth.

Kente cloth is much more than just a piece of cloth – it is a symbol of Ghanaian cultural heritage and history. From its origins in the Ashanti kingdom to its role in political activism, Kente cloth continues to hold a special place in the hearts of Ghanaians. Whether worn on special occasions or displayed as a work of art, Kente cloth is a testament to the rich cultural heritage of Ghana.

To fly to Ghana from the west you will need to have a valid passport containing empty pages and at least 6 months past your arrival and departure from that country, in this case, Ghana.

To apply for a U.S. passport, you need to submit the following items:

1. A completed passport application (Form DS-11).
2. A 2-inch by 2-inch passport photo taken within the last 6 months.
3. Your current U.S. passport (if applicable).
4. Proof of U.S. citizenship, such as a birth certificate or naturalization certificate.
5. Proof of identity, such as a government-issued photo ID (e.g. driver's license).
6. Payment for the application fee and any expedited services needed.

★ **If you are a first-time passport applicant** or your previous passport was lost or stolen, you will need to apply in person at a U.S. Department of State agency or U.S. Passport Acceptance Facility. If you have had a passport before, you may be eligible to renew by mail.

Find yourself needing to come to Ghana in an emergency? Abususa Travels provides visa-on-arrival services. Please reach out to us via email or telephone to pre-register for Visa-on-Arrival Services through Abusua Travels. Abusua means Family!

Customs

U.S. Customs and Border Protection (CBP) is the federal agency responsible for securing the country's borders and enforcing U.S. customs laws. CBP officers are stationed at airports and other points of entry into the United States to inspect and process travelers and their belongings as they enter the country. The agency's mission is to protect the American people, facilitate legitimate trade and travel, and prevent the entry of harmful people and goods into the United States.

At airports, CBP officers inspect travelers' passports and visas and verify their eligibility to enter the country. They may ask travelers questions about their travel plans, including their reasons for traveling outside the United States and their intended length of stay. If they suspect that a traveler may be carrying prohibited or restricted items, they may inspect their luggage, carry-on bags, or personal belongings.

While inspecting travelers is the main duty, CBP also inspects goods that are being imported into the United States. CBP officers work to ensure that the goods being brought from country to country comply with U.S. laws and regulations. They may check for contraband, prohibited items, or counterfeit goods, and seize any items that are found to violate U.S. law on your return.

CBP also has a responsibility to protect public health and safety. For example, they may inspect food, plants, and animals being brought into the United States to ensure that they are free from pests and diseases that could harm American agriculture or public health. <u>Never bring back any organic material that is prohibited.</u>

Overall, the role of CBP at airports is to protect the security and integrity of the United States. By inspecting travelers and their belongings, they help ensure that only those who are eligible and have a legitimate reason for entering the country are allowed to do so. By inspecting imported goods, they help prevent harmful items from entering the country and protect American businesses and consumers. When you are traveling to or from the United States, it is important to familiarize yourself with the country's customs laws and procedures and to be prepared for inspection by Immigration or Environmental Protection officers.

CDC Travel Medicine

If you're planning on traveling outside of the United States, it's important to take steps to protect your health. One of these steps is to schedule a travel medicine appointment with the Centers for Disease Control and Prevention (CDC).

What you can expect during a CDC travel medicine appointment:

Consultation: The first step of the appointment is a consultation with a healthcare provider. They will ask you questions about your travel plans, including the destinations you plan to visit, the length of your stay, and any specific activities you plan to engage in.

Health assessment: The healthcare provider will then perform a health assessment to determine if you are at risk for any illnesses that are common in the areas you plan to visit. This may include a review of your current health status, any pre-existing medical conditions, and any immunizations you have received in the past.

Vaccination recommendations: Based on your travel plans and health assessment, the healthcare provider will make recommendations for any vaccinations you may need. This may include vaccines for diseases such as yellow fever, polio, or typhoid.

Medications: If you are traveling to a destination where there is a risk of malaria, the healthcare provider may prescribe antimalarial medications. They may also recommend other medications for the prevention of traveler's diarrhea or altitude sickness, depending on your travel plans.

Information about health risks: The healthcare provider will also provide you with information about any health risks you may face while traveling, including advice on how to protect yourself from diseases and how to seek medical attention if necessary.

Follow-up: Before leaving on your trip, it's a good idea to schedule a follow-up appointment to make sure you have received all the necessary vaccinations and medications.

By scheduling a travel medicine appointment with the CDC, you can take steps to protect your health while traveling. The healthcare provider will work with you to develop a personalized travel health plan, taking into account your travel plans, health status, and any other factors that may impact your health while traveling. So, if you're planning on traveling abroad, be sure to schedule a CDC travel medicine appointment as soon as possible.

List of recommended inoculations:

The recommended inoculations for traveling to Ghana may vary depending on individual factors such as age, health status, and itinerary. However, some of the commonly recommended vaccinations for travelers to Ghana include:

- Yellow fever
- Hepatitis A and B
- Typhoid fever
- Meningococcal disease
- Measles, mumps, and rubella (MMR)
- Polio
- Rabies

It is recommended to consult with a healthcare provider or travel medicine a specialist at least 4-6 weeks before the trip to discuss specific vaccination needs and other health considerations.

Yellow fever

Yellow fever is an acute viral illness that is transmitted by mosquitoes. It is caused by the yellow fever virus and is most commonly found in tropical areas of Africa and South America. The symptoms of yellow fever include fever, headache, muscle aches, and jaundice (yellowing of the skin and eyes). In severe cases, yellow fever can lead to liver and kidney failure, and even death.

Yellow fever is diagnosed based on the symptoms and a person's travel history. There is currently no specific treatment for yellow fever, but early supportive care can help reduce the severity of symptoms and prevent complications. This may include hydration, pain relief, and medications to manage fever. In addition, a yellow fever vaccine is available and is highly recommended for travelers to areas where yellow fever is common.

It is important to take precautions to avoid mosquito bites when traveling to areas where yellow fever is present. This may include wearing long sleeves and pants, using insect repellent, and staying in air-conditioned or well-screened buildings. It is also important to follow guidelines for avoiding mosquito bites when living in areas where yellow fever is common, such as using insecticide sprays, sleeping under mosquito nets, and avoiding standing water where mosquitoes breed.

By taking these steps, individuals can reduce their risk of contracting yellow fever and help prevent the spread of the disease. Yellow fever is an acute viral illness that can cause a range of symptoms. The following are some of the most common symptoms of yellow fever:

1. **Fever:** This is one of the most prominent symptoms of yellow fever, and is typically accompanied by chills, sweating, and weakness.
2. **Headache:** Many people with yellow fever experience headaches, which can be severe and persistent.
3. **Muscle aches:** Muscle aches and pain are common symptoms of yellow fever, especially in the back, legs, and arms.
4. **Jaundice:** Yellowing of the skin and eyes (jaundice) is a hallmark of yellow fever and is caused by the buildup of bilirubin in the bloodstream.
5. **Nausea and vomiting:** Some people with yellow fever experience nausea and vomiting, which can be severe and persistent.
6. **Fatigue:** Yellow fever can cause significant fatigue, making it difficult for individuals to carry out their daily activities.
7. **Abdominal pain:** Some people with yellow fever experience abdominal pain, which can be caused by the inflammation of the liver or other organs.

It's important to note that not everyone with yellow fever will experience all of these symptoms, and some individuals may only have mild symptoms, while others may develop more severe symptoms that require medical treatment. If you suspect you have yellow fever, it's important to see a healthcare provider as soon as possible.

Malaria

Preventing malaria in a developing country is a critical challenge, as the disease continues to cause significant morbidity and mortality in these areas. Fortunately, several measures can be taken to reduce the incidence of malaria and protect individuals from this potentially life-threatening illness.

One of the most important steps in preventing malaria is controlling the mosquito population. This can be achieved through the use of insecticide-treated bed nets or clothing, which provide a protective barrier against mosquito bites while individuals are sleeping. Indoor residual sprays, which contain insecticides, can be used to kill mosquitoes on contact and reduce the number of mosquitoes in the home.

Another important step in preventing malaria is promoting the use of antimalarial drugs. These medications can be used prophylactically to prevent malaria, or they can be used to treat the illness once it has been diagnosed. If you experience any signs or symptoms of malaria, it's important to promptly seek medical treatment. Ensure that you are aware of the measures that can be taken to prevent malaria.

Preventing malaria in a developing country requires a multi-faceted approach, including controlling the mosquito population, promoting the use of antimalarial drugs, and educating yourself about the potential for disease and how to prevent it. By taking these steps, you can work towards reducing the incidence of contracting malaria during your visit.

Search the CDC Website for clinics in your state here:

[CDC Travel Health- Find a Clinic](#)

Link to CDC Traveler's Health:

Chapter 4: Shopping and Dining in Ghana

Shopping

Shopping at street markets in Africa can be an exciting and new experience. The markets are usually filled with vendors selling a wide range of products, from fresh produce and spices to handmade crafts and textiles. The atmosphere is lively, with vendors calling out to attract customers, music playing, and the hustle and bustle of people bargaining for goods.

In many African markets, bargaining is a common practice and part of the shopping experience. You can expect to haggle with vendors over prices, but it's important to keep in mind that haggling should be done in a friendly and respectful manner. The prices in these markets can be lower than in traditional shops, but it's important to keep an eye on the quality of the products.

The fresh produce on offer at street markets in Africa is often of high quality and sold at a fraction of the cost of what you would find in supermarkets. You can find a variety of indigenous fruits, and vegetables, as well as spices like curry, cumin, and coriander, some of which may not be available in other parts of the world. The markets also offer a great opportunity to try new and local foods, including street food stalls that sell traditional dishes.

From intricate beadwork and hand-woven baskets to colorful clothing and pottery, there is a lot to see and explore. Shopping at these markets is also a great way to support local artisans and small businesses.

Overall, shopping at street markets in Africa is a unique and memorable experience that offers a glimpse into local culture and traditions. Whether you're looking for fresh produce, handmade goods, or just a fun day out, a visit to one of these markets is sure to be an unforgettable adventure.

Price Haggling at Makola Market

Makola Market in Accra, Ghana is one of the largest street markets in West Africa and a popular tourist destination. It is a bustling hub of activity, with vendors selling everything from fresh produce and spices to textiles and handmade crafts. The market is known for its atmosphere, with vendors calling out to attract customers, music playing, and the sounds of bargaining and haggling filling the air.

Makola Market is the world's largest bazaar located in the heart of Accra, the capital city of Ghana. It is considered one of the largest and most vibrant markets in West Africa and a must-visit destination for anyone traveling to Ghana. The market is a hive of activity, where locals and tourists alike come to purchase goods and provisions like traditional textiles and crafts to modern electronics and household items.

One of the highlights of shopping at Makola Market is the vast amount of goods on offer. Fresh produce is abundant, and the spices and herbs on offer are of high quality. Visitors can also find a range of traditional textiles, including kente cloth and batik, mud cloth, handmade jewelry and shoes as well as the infamous Africa Sponge, to intricate and traditional beadwork and pottery.

Bargaining is a common practice at Makola Market, and visitors are expected to haggle with vendors over prices. While the prices can be lower than in traditional shops, it is important to keep an eye on the quality of the products and to be aware of any potential scams.

However, shopping at Makola Market is also an opportunity to support local artisans and small businesses, and visitors can often find unique and one-of-a-kind items that cannot be found anywhere else. Whether you are looking for fresh produce, handmade goods, or just a fun day out, a visit to Makola Market is a must-see for anyone visiting Accra, Ghana.

The market is a labyrinth of narrow alleyways, lined with colorful stalls and vendors selling everything from spices, herbs, and foodstuffs, to clothing, jewelry, and beauty products. The air is filled with the sounds of bargaining, haggling, and laughter, and the colorful displays of goods are sure to capture the attention of any shopper.

As you enter the market, you are greeted by a sea of lively colors and the irresistible aroma of spices and traditional foods. The first thing you will notice is the frenzied energy of the vendors, who are constantly shouting out to attract customers to their stalls. It's not uncommon to be approached by several vendors at once, each eager to show you their wares.

One of the highlights of shopping at Makola Market is the opportunity to purchase traditional textiles, including the famous Kente cloth. Kente is a symbol of Ghanaian heritage and is often worn on special occasions. The market is a great place to find authentic Kente cloth, made by local artisans, in a range of styles and designs.

While offering a plethora of traditional textiles, the market is also a great place to purchase handmade crafts and souvenirs, such as hand-carved wooden masks, beaded jewelry, and traditional baskets. These items are not only beautiful but also make for unique gifts or keepsakes to bring back home.

For those interested in more practical purchases, Makola Market is also a hub for electronics and household goods. You can find everything from smartphones and laptops to kitchen appliances and tools. The market is a great place to find affordable prices, don't be afraid to haggle and negotiate, as is expected in the market culture.

Shopping at Makola Market in Accra is an experience that should not be missed by anyone visiting Ghana. The market is a feast for the senses, whether you're looking for souvenirs, gifts, or simply a unique shopping experience, Makola Market is sure to deliver.

Duty-Free Shopping

Duty-free shopping has been a popular way to save money on luxury items and travel essentials for many years. With a growing number of airports and borders offering duty-free shopping options, it's no wonder why more and more people are taking advantage of this convenient way to save money while traveling. Here are just a few of the many benefits of duty-free shopping.

1. **No Taxes or Duties:** One of the biggest draws of duty-free shopping is the fact that you don't have to pay taxes or duties on your purchases. This can result in significant savings, especially when buying luxury items like jewelry, watches, or high-end electronics.

2. **Wider Selection:** Duty-free shops often carry a wider selection of items than traditional retail stores, and you can find items from all over the world. This makes it easier to find that perfect item you're looking for, or to discover new products that you may not have had access to before.

3. **Convenient and Time-Saving:**
Shopping for luxury items at a duty-free
shop can be a very convenient and
time-saving experience. Many duty-free
shops are located in airports, making
them accessible to travelers without
having to leave the airport. And since
they are often open 24/7, you can shop
whenever it's convenient for you.

4. **Competitive Pricing:** Due to the lack of
taxes and duties, duty-free shops are
often able to offer competitive pricing on
items. This can result in substantial
savings compared to traditional retail
stores, making it an excellent option for
those who are budget-conscious.

5. **Exclusivity:** Shopping at a duty-free
shop can be a luxurious and exclusive
experience. With a wide range of
high-end products and a sophisticated
shopping atmosphere, you can feel like
you're getting something special when
you make a purchase.

Duty-free shopping is an excellent way to save money, discover new products, and enjoy a luxurious shopping experience. Whether you're looking for luxury items, travel essentials, or just want to save money on your next trip, duty-free shopping is an excellent option to consider. So the next time you travel, be sure to take advantage of this fantastic opportunity to save money and get more for your money.

Extended layovers at International airports are a great way to get that high-end good you have had your eye on. Be sure to add time to browse and shop to your itinerary.

★

Declaration Forms

Declaring goods to customs is an important part of the duty-free shopping process. When entering a country, travelers are required to declare any goods that they have purchased abroad and may be subject to duties and taxes. Failing to declare goods to customs can result in serious consequences, including fines, seizure of the goods, and even legal action.

To declare goods to customs, travelers must fill out a declaration form, which can usually be obtained at the airport or border crossing. The form will ask for information such as the type of goods being declared, their value, and the country of origin. It's important to be truthful and accurate when filling out the form, as providing false information can result in serious penalties.

In addition to the declaration form, travelers may also be required to present their receipts or proof of purchase for the goods they are declaring. This is to ensure that the items being declared match the information provided on the form, and to verify that the goods were indeed purchased duty-free. After the declaration form and proof of purchase have been submitted, customs officials will determine whether the goods are eligible for duty-free status and if so, the traveler can proceed through customs with their purchases.

Declaring goods to customs is an important step in the duty-free shopping process, and travelers should be familiar with the rules and regulations regarding customs declarations. By being honest and accurate when declaring goods to customs, travelers can avoid any potential problems and enjoy the benefits of duty-free shopping.

★ **Always print and use - BLOCK CAPITAL letters when filling out government and international forms.**

Dining in Accra

While shopping at Makola Market seize the opportunity to sample the local street food. The market is home to a wide range of food stalls, offering everything from spicy stews and fried plantains to grilled chicken and traditional rice dishes. These dishes are not only delicious but also provide a glimpse into the rich culinary heritage of Ghana. Street food stalls, known locally as "Chop bars" offer a chance to sample traditional dishes, such as jollof rice and waakye. The traditional Ghanaian spices will be calling to you through dishes like Light Soup, Okro Stew, Banku, and Kenkey which are local staples. If you are an adventurous eater ask for the snails or Grasscutter stew!

Accra is known for its effervescent, contemporary history, and diverse cuisine. The city offers a plethora of dining options, including street food stalls, local eateries, and upscale restaurants. Fine dining in Accra has become a popular trend, with many restaurants offering sophisticated menus, exceptional service, and a luxurious ambiance.

A popular fine dining establishment in Accra is Ophelia's. This upscale restaurant offers a fusion of Mediterranean and African flavors, featuring a menu that includes grilled lamb chops, pan-seared salmon, and slow-roasted chicken. The dining room is spacious and elegantly decorated, featuring large windows that allow natural light to flood the room.

For those looking for a more traditional African dining experience, the Africa House Restaurant is an excellent choice. This restaurant features a menu that showcases the diverse flavors of Africa, with dishes such as jollof rice, plantains, and goat stew. The restaurant's interior is decorated with animated African textiles and paintings, creating a lively and energetic atmosphere.

Accra offers a thriving fine dining scene, with a variety of restaurants that offer exceptional cuisine, exceptional service, and a luxurious ambiance. Whether you are in the mood for contemporary French cuisine, fusion cooking, or traditional African dishes, there is a fine dining restaurant in Accra that is sure to satisfy your cravings. So, if you are looking for a sophisticated dining experience in Accra, be sure to try one of the city's many fine dining establishments.

You will be surprised to find some of your favorites from back home in Accra as well. Don't miss out on going to the Accra Mall, The Achimota Mall, The Marina Mall, or the China Mall to find some of your favorite comfort foods from back home like hot wings, burgers and fries, and warm mac n cheese while you are on your trip to Ghana.

Ghanaian Cuisine: A Celebration of Bold Flavors and Aromatic Spices

Ghanaian cuisine is a delicious and diverse blend of traditional West African dishes, European and American influences, and a mix of regional cooking styles. The food of Ghana is characterized by its use of bold spices, fresh ingredients, and unique flavor combinations that have been passed down through generations.

One of the defining features of Ghanaian cuisine is the use of spices. The most commonly used spices in Ghanaian cooking include ginger, garlic, allspice, nutmeg, black pepper, cinnamon, and cardamom. These spices are used to add depth, heat, and a subtle sweetness to dishes, and are often combined in unique ways to create complex yet satisfying flavors.

The two sisters- Ginger is a staple ingredient in Ghanaian cooking and is used in a variety of dishes, from soups and stews to stir-fries and marinades. Fresh ginger adds a slightly spicy and pungent flavor to dishes, while dried ginger is often used for its warm, sweet aroma. Garlic is another important ingredient in Ghanaian cooking and is used to add depth and richness to dishes

Allspice, also known as Jamaica pepper, is a unique spice that combines the flavors of cinnamon, nutmeg, and cloves. It is often used in savory dishes, such as stews and soups, to add a warm and sweet aroma to the dish. Black pepper is a staple in Ghanaian cooking and is used to add heat and a slightly pungent flavor to dishes. From spicy stews to marinades, black pepper is an essential ingredient in Ghanaian cooking.

Nutmeg is another versatile spice that is commonly used in Ghanaian cuisine. With its sweet and slightly spicy flavor, nutmeg is often used to add depth and complexity to sauces, soups, and stews. In Ghana, you will find locals flavoring their morning oats with plenty of delicious nutmeg.

Cinnamon is a warm, sweet spice that is often used in sweet dishes and baked goods. Ghanaian cuisine is also used to add depth and flavor to savory dishes, such as stews and soups. Cardamom is a sweet and slightly spicy spice that is often used in sweets and baked goods, such as cakes and bread, and savory dishes, such as stews and curries.

Ghanaian cuisine is a delicious and diverse celebration of bold flavors and aromatic spices. The spices used in Ghanaian cooking are carefully selected and combined to create complex and satisfying dishes that have been enjoyed for generations.

Old World, New Flavors

The flavors and spices used in Ghanaian cuisine are not limited to West Africa and have also made a significant impact on Caribbean and American cuisine, particularly in the form of soul food. The large West African influence on the Caribbean and the Americas shows the ancestors brought their culinary traditions with them.

Over time, their traditional dishes were adapted and blended with local ingredients, resulting in the creation of unique and flavorful cuisines from Peru and Columbia, and Panama to New Orleans, The Gulluh Geechee Coast, and beyond.

In the Caribbean, spices such as allspice, nutmeg, and cinnamon, share roots in West African cooking and have been used to flavor meat, vegetables, and sauces. The spicy and aromatic flavors of these spices have been incorporated into traditional Caribbean dishes, such as jerk chicken, curried goat, and rice and peas, adding depth and complexity to the dishes.

In America, African and Caribbean influences have had a significant impact on soul food. The use of spices such as ginger, garlic, black pepper, and allspice has become a hallmark of this cuisine, with these ingredients being used to flavor dishes such as shepherds pie, collard greens, and black-eyed peas, which you will find a similarity to Ghanaian Red-Red. The use of spices in soul food reflects the West African and Caribbean heritage of many African Americans and has become a defining characteristic of this cuisine.

The spices and flavors used in Ghanaian cuisine have made a significant impact on Caribbean and American cuisine, particularly in the form of comfort foods. The use of bold and aromatic spices, such as ginger, garlic, allspice, nutmeg, black pepper, cinnamon, and cardamom, has become a staple in these cuisines, bringing a full circle moment to traditional dishes and reflecting the rich cultural heritage and deep connection of West African and Caribbean-American communities.

Jerk Soul Restaurant: A Fusion of Caribbean and West African Cuisine

In the Oyarifa area, before the lush Aburi Hills, just a short drive from Accra, Ghana, is a restaurant that offers a unique dining experience. Jerk Soul, owned and operated by Telie Woods, provides a fusion of Caribbean and Soul Food cuisine that delights the taste buds and warms the soul.

The menu at Jerk Soul features a range of dishes that combine the flavors and ingredients of the Caribbean and West Africa. From the spicy and aromatic jerk chicken to the tomato-rich jollof rice, each dish is a celebration; of the diverse culinary traditions that have influenced the Americas.

One of the signature dishes at Jerk Soul is the plantain and black bean stew, which combines the sweetness of ripe plantains with the earthiness of black beans and the warmth of African spices. Another popular dish is the coconut curry shrimp, which features succulent shrimp cooked in a fragrant blend of Caribbean and West local spices, with creamy coconut milk tying it all together.

The owner of Jerk Soul, Telie Woods, is a visionary entrepreneur who is passionate about sharing the beauty of Ghanaian cuisine with the world. Born and raised in the United States, Woods has always been interested in exploring his African heritage and connecting with the continent.

Since its opening, Jerk Soul has become a meeting place for African Americans traveling to Ghana. Visitors to the restaurant come to connect with other people from the diaspora and share their experiences of returning to the continent. The restaurant has become a hub of cultural exchange, where people from different backgrounds can come together and celebrate the diversity of African cuisine and culture.

In addition to its innovative menu, Jerk Soul also offers a welcoming and relaxed atmosphere that makes diners feel at home. The restaurant's open-air design allows patrons to enjoy the stunning views of the Aburi Hills while dining on delicious food. The staff is friendly and accommodating, and the restaurant's overall ambiance is warm and inviting.

One of the standout features of Jerk Soul is its rooftop location. Situated atop a hill in a mall, the restaurant offers breathtaking panoramic views of the surrounding landscape and offers underground parking which is a treat! The open-air design of the rooftop allows diners to enjoy the refreshing breeze and natural beauty of the area while they savor their delicious food.

The rooftop location adds to the overall ambiance of the restaurant. The bright and colorful decor, combined with the lush greenery and stunning views create an energetic atmosphere. Diners can kickback, relax and take in the sights and sounds of the surrounding area while enjoying their food and company.

Jerk Soul's rooftop location has also become a popular spot for events and gatherings. The restaurant can accommodate large groups and hosts a variety of events, including live music performances, private parties, and weddings.

The rooftop is also an opportunity for taking photos and capturing memories of the beautiful views and surroundings. The restaurants photo conscious design lends some unique views as well dont forget to get pix your friends will envy!

Jerk Soul is a restaurant that offers a unique and exciting culinary experience. Through its fusion of both Caribbean and West African cuisine, Jerk Soul celebrates the richness and diversity of global African culture.

As a meeting place for Africans from the Americans, the Caribbean and Europe returning to Ghana, it provides a space for people to connect and share their experiences. If you are ever in Accra, be sure to pay a visit to Jerk Soul and experience the magic for yourself.

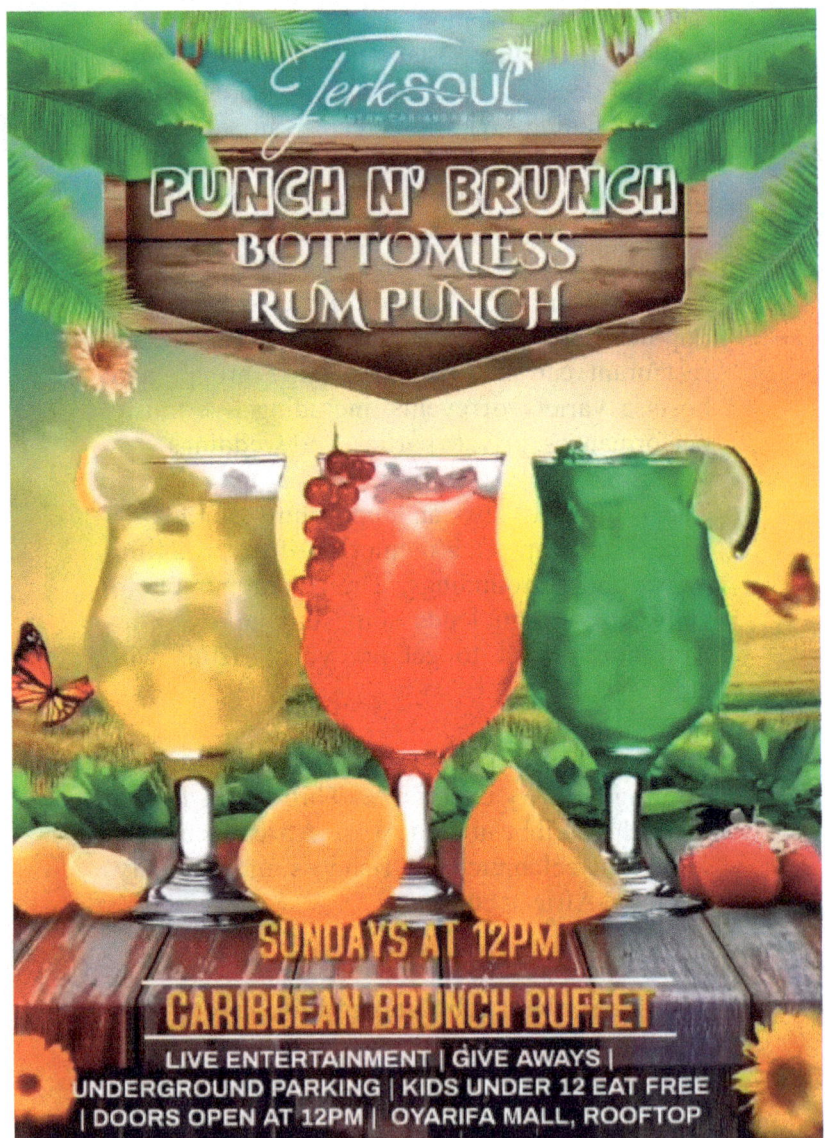

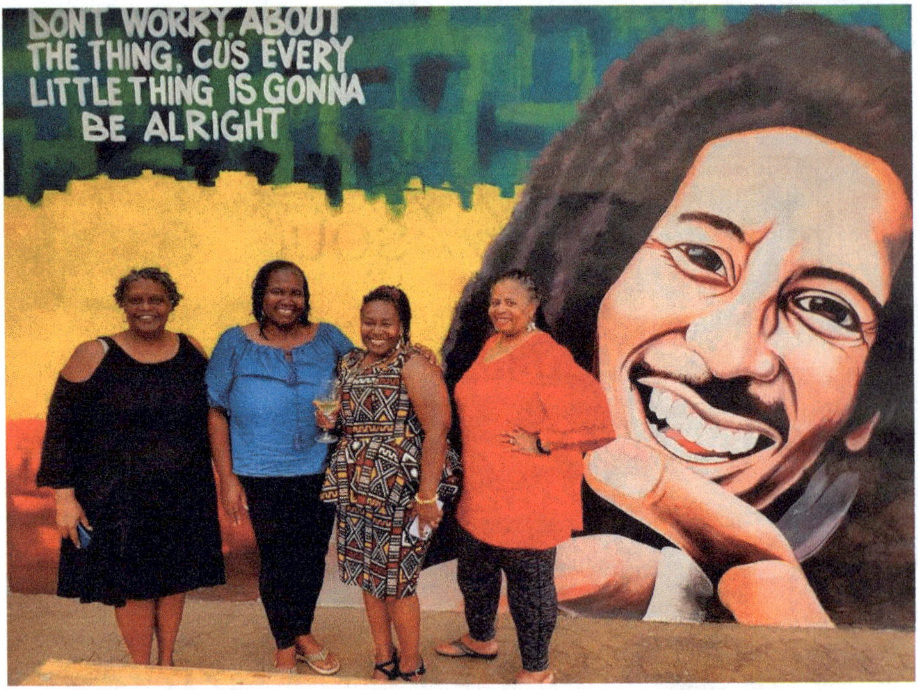
DON'T WORRY ABOUT
THE THING, CUS EVERY
LITTLE THING IS GONNA
BE ALRIGHT

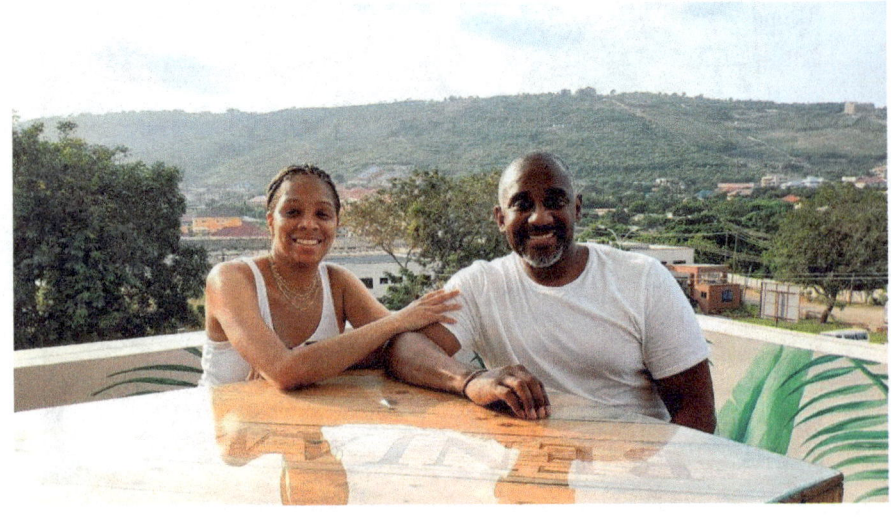

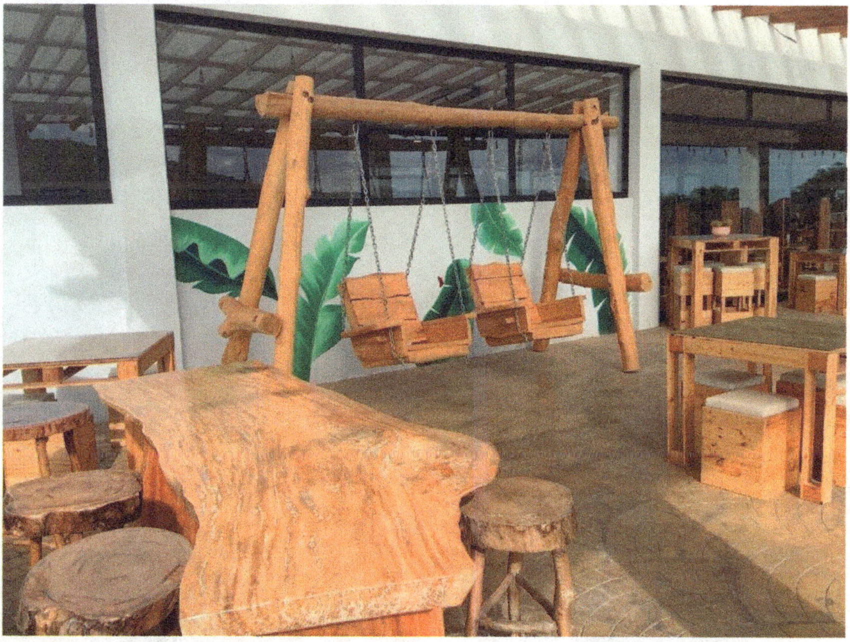

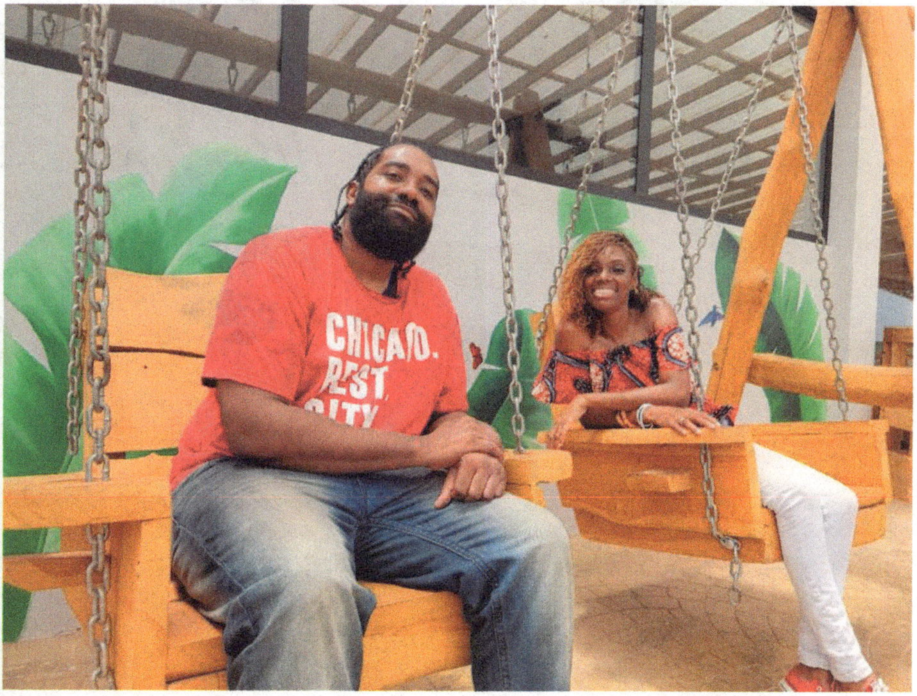
CHICAGO.

Chapter 5: NIghtlife and Excursions

Accra, is known for its high-spirited nightlife. The city boasts a wide range of entertainment options, from music clubs to bars and restaurants. This chapter will explore the nightlife scene in Accra, including popular spots, music genres, and cultural activities.

One of the most popular areas for nightlife in Accra is Osu, known as the "Oxford Street" of Ghana. Here you will find a range of bars, clubs, and restaurants to choose from. Some of the popular spots in Osu include Carbon, Bloom Bar, and Twist Nightclub. These clubs often feature local and international DJs playing a variety of music genres, including hip-hop, afrobeats, and dancehall.

Other areas in Accra also offer nightlife options. For example, Labone is known for its upscale lounges and rooftop bars, while East Legon is home to several sports bars and pubs. The beaches of Accra are also popular spots for nightlife, with many bars and restaurants offering live music and other entertainment.

A unique features of Accra's nightlife scene is the emphasis on cultural activities. Many venues feature live performances by local artists, including traditional drumming and dancing. Additionally, you can find events that highlight Ghanaian culture, such as poetry readings and storytelling sessions.

When it comes to music, afrobeats is a dominant genre in Accra's nightlife scene. This upbeat, danceable music style originated in West Africa and has gained global popularity in recent years. Other popular genres include highlife, hiplife, and reggae. Many clubs and bars also feature live music performances by local artists, providing a platform for up-and-coming musicians to showcase their talent.

In terms of dress code, most nightlife spots in Accra have a smart casual dress code. This means you can wear comfortable, stylish clothes without being too formal. However, some clubs may have a stricter dress code, so it's always a good idea to check before you go.

Overall, the nightlife scene in Accra offers a diverse range of entertainment options, with something for everyone. Whether you're looking to dance the night away, enjoy live music, or experience local culture, you're sure to find it in this bustling and electrifying city.

Places to Stay & Play!

Accra Neighborhoods

Greater Accra is Ghana's largest city, with a population of over 4 million people. The city is a melting pot of cultures and traditions, making it a hub of diversity and innovation. As the city continues to grow, new neighborhoods are emerging, each with its unique character and flavor. Here are seven popular neighborhoods in Greater Accra worth paying a visit to.

East Legon Hills

East Legon Hills is a fast-growing residential area located in the northern part of Accra. It is known for its serene and peaceful environment, making it a popular choice for families and young professionals. The neighborhood has easy access to major highways and is a short drive from the airport. With a mix of modern and traditional architecture, East Legon Hills is quickly becoming one of the most sought-after neighborhoods in Greater Accra.

Adenta

Adenta is a vivacious neighborhood located in the eastern part of Accra. It is a bustling commercial and residential area with a mix of modern and traditional architecture. The neighborhood is well-connected to the city's major highways and is home to several international schools, making it a popular choice for families. Adenta is also home to several shopping centers and markets, making it a great place for shopping and entertainment.

Dansoman

Dansoman is a lively neighborhood located in the western part of Accra. It is a densely populated area with a mix of residential and commercial properties. The neighborhood has a rich cultural heritage and is home to several historic landmarks, including the Ghana National Cultural Centre. With its busy markets, restaurants, and shops, Dansoman is an excellent place to experience the local Ghanaian culture.

East Legon

East Legon is a trendy and upscale neighborhood located in the northern part of Accra. It is known for its luxurious properties, high-end restaurants, and designer boutiques. The neighborhood is a popular choice for ex-pats and wealthy Ghanaians, with some of the city's most exclusive properties located here. East Legon also has excellent schools, making it an ideal location for families.

Spintex Road

Spintex Road is a rapidly developing neighborhood located in the eastern part of Accra. It is a popular commercial and residential area with a mix of modern and traditional architecture. The neighborhood has excellent road connectivity and is home to several shopping centers, restaurants, and hotels. Spintex Road is also known for its thriving nightlife, with several bars and clubs located in the area.

Airport Residential Area

The Airport Residential Area is a prestigious neighborhood located in the northern part of Accra. It is a highly sought-after residential area, with several embassies and international organizations located in the area. The neighborhood is just minutes to the city's major highways and is home to several high-end restaurants and shops. With its tranquil environment and luxurious properties, the Airport Residential Area is a great place to live for those who can afford it.

Osu

Osu is a dynamic and cosmopolitan neighborhood located in the central part of Accra. It is a popular commercial and entertainment hub with a mix of modern and traditional architecture. The neighborhood is home to several international restaurants, bars, and nightclubs, making it a popular destination for tourists and locals alike. Osu is also known for its street art and cultural landmarks, including the Osu Castle and the Kwame Nkrumah Memorial Park.

Greater Accra is a city that is constantly evolving, and these seven neighborhoods are just a few examples of the exciting changes taking place. Each of these neighborhoods has its unique character and offers something different for residents and visitors. As the city continues to grow, we can expect to see many more well-situated, colorful, and bright neighborhoods emerge, each with its own unique flavor and style.

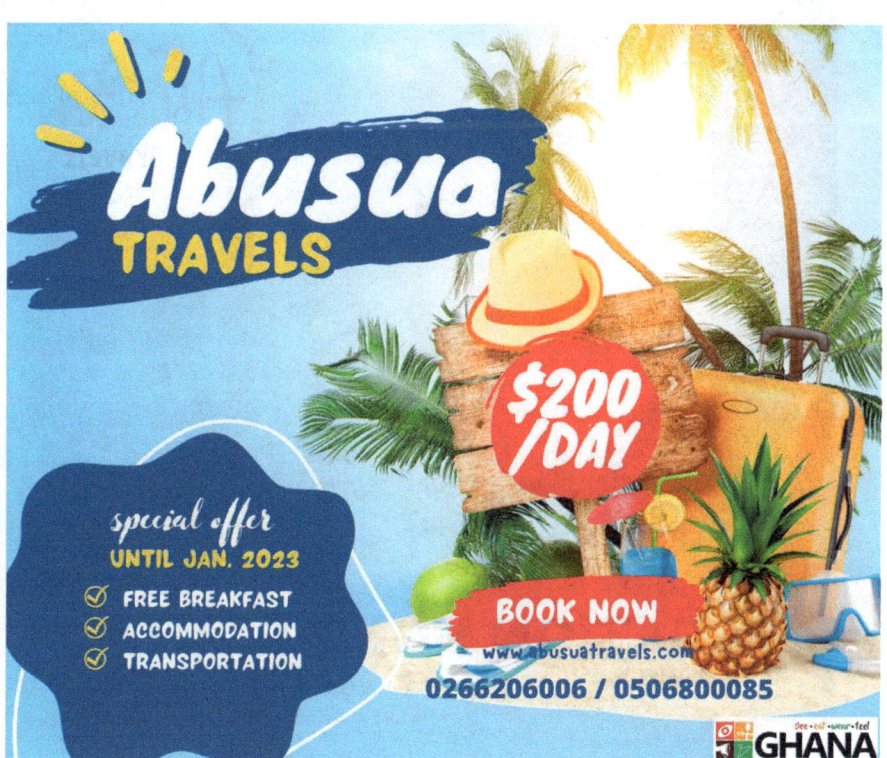

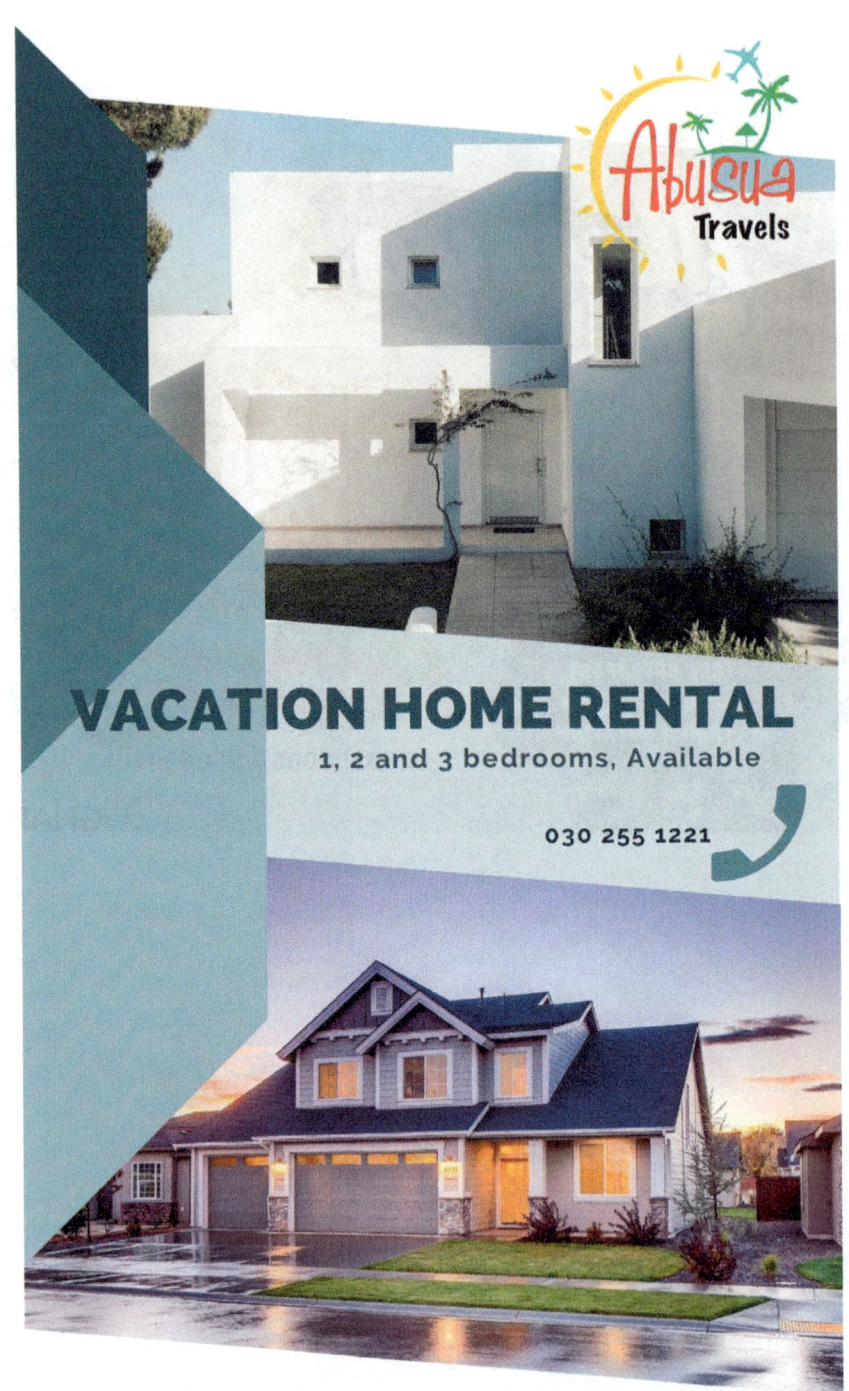

VACATION HOME RENTAL

1, 2 and 3 bedrooms, Available

030 255 1221

www.abusuatavels.com

Places to Play!

Explore the Kakum National Park

If you're a nature lover, the Kakum National Park is a must-visit destination. It is home to over 40 different species of mammals, including forest elephants, forest buffalo, and antelopes. The park is also famous for its canopy walkway, which is suspended 30 meters above the ground. It is a thrilling experience to walk on the canopy walkway and see the rainforest from a bird's eye view.

Take a trip to the Volta Region

The Volta Region is located in the eastern part of Ghana and is known for its scenic beauty. The region is home to the Volta River, which is the longest river in West Africa. The river offers a great opportunity for water activities such as swimming, kayaking, and canoeing. The region is also home to the Wli Waterfalls, which is the highest waterfall in West Africa.

Learn about the Ashanti Kingdom

The Ashanti Kingdom is one of the most significant kingdoms in Ghana's history. The kingdom was known for its wealth and power, and it played a significant role in the transatlantic slave trade. A visit to the Manhyia Palace Museum in Kumasi will give you a glimpse into the history and culture of the Ashanti people.

Relax on the Beaches

Ghana has some of the most beautiful beaches in West Africa. The beaches are perfect for relaxation and water sports. Some of the popular beaches in Ghana include Labadi Beach, Kokrobite Beach, and Busua Beach. You can enjoy swimming, sunbathing, and surfing on these beaches.

Take a trip to the Volta Region

The Volta Region is located in the eastern part of Ghana and is known for its scenic beauty. The region is home to the Volta River, which is the longest river in West Africa. The river offers a great opportunity for water activities such as swimming, kayaking, and canoeing. The region is also home to the Wli Waterfalls, which is the highest waterfall in West Africa.

Learn about the Ashanti Kingdom

The Ashanti Kingdom is one of the most significant kingdoms in Ghana's history. The kingdom was known for its wealth and power, and it played a significant role in the transatlantic slave trade. A visit to the Manhyia Palace Museum in Kumasi will give you a glimpse into the history and culture of the Ashanti people.

Relax on the Beaches (cont.)

Ghana has some of the most beautiful beaches in West Africa. The beaches are perfect for relaxation and water sports. Some of the popular beaches in Ghana include Labadi Beach, Kokrobite Beach, and Busua Beach. You can enjoy swimming, sunbathing, and surfing on these beaches.

Ghana is a great destination for tourists who want to experience the rich culture and natural beauty of West Africa. In this chapter, we have highlighted some of the best excursions to take in Ghana. From historical tours to nature walks, Ghana has something to offer everyone. So pack your bags and get ready for an exciting adventure in Ghana.

Pristine Beaches in Ghana - Cape Coast, Elmina, and the Volta Region

Ghana is a country located in West Africa, bordered by Côte d'Ivoire to the west, Burkina Faso to the north, Togo to the east, and the Gulf of Guinea to the south. The country is known for its rich culture, history, and stunning natural beauty, including its many pristine beaches.

In this chapter, we will explore some of the most beautiful beaches in Ghana, located in the coastal towns of Cape Coast and Elmina, as well as the Volta Region.

Cape Coast

Cape Coast is a historic town located in the Central Region of Ghana, known for its role in the transatlantic slave trade. However, it is also home to some of the most beautiful beaches in the country, including the popular Brenu Beach.

Brenu Beach is a pristine stretch of sand that runs for several miles along the Atlantic Ocean. It is known for its crystal-clear waters and soft, white sand. Visitors can relax on the beach, swim in the ocean, or take a stroll along the coastline.

Another beautiful beach in Cape Coast is the Oasis Beach Resort. This beach resort features a private beach, lush gardens, and comfortable accommodations. Visitors can enjoy a range of activities, including beach volleyball, kayaking, and swimming.

Elmina

Elmina is another historic town located in the Central Region of Ghana, famous for its beautiful beaches and the Elmina Castle, a UNESCO World Heritage Site. One of the most popular beaches in Elmina is the Coconut Grove Beach Resort.

Local resorts offer a range of accommodations, from cozy beach huts to luxurious villas. Visitors can enjoy swimming in the ocean, relaxing on the beach, or taking part in water sports.

Another beautiful beach in Elmina is the Biriwa Beach. This beach is known for its serene atmosphere, crystal-clear waters, and soft, white sand. Visitors can enjoy swimming, sunbathing, or taking a stroll along the coastline.

Elmina has become a popular destination due to its proximity in the Centtral Region of the country. The distance is just right for a day or two excursion.

Volta Region

The Volta Region is located in the eastern part of Ghana, known for its beautiful landscapes, including mountains, waterfalls, and beaches.

Ada Foah Beach is a tranquil oasis, located on the banks of the Volta River. The beach is known for its calm waters and soft, white sand. Visitors can relax on the beach, take a dip in the river, or explore the nearby mangrove forests.

Another beautiful beach in the Volta Region is the Keta Beach. This beach is known for its open atmosphere, featuring colorful beach huts, lively music, and delicious street food. Visitors can enjoy swimming, sunbathing, or taking a walk along the sunny coast.

Ghana is home to some of the most beautiful beaches in Africa, located in coastal towns from Cape Coast to the Volta Region. These beaches offer visitors a chance to relax, unwind, and soak up the natural beauty of the country. From the soft, white sands of Brenu Beach to the crystal-clear waters of Keta, there is a beach in Ghana to suit every taste and preference.

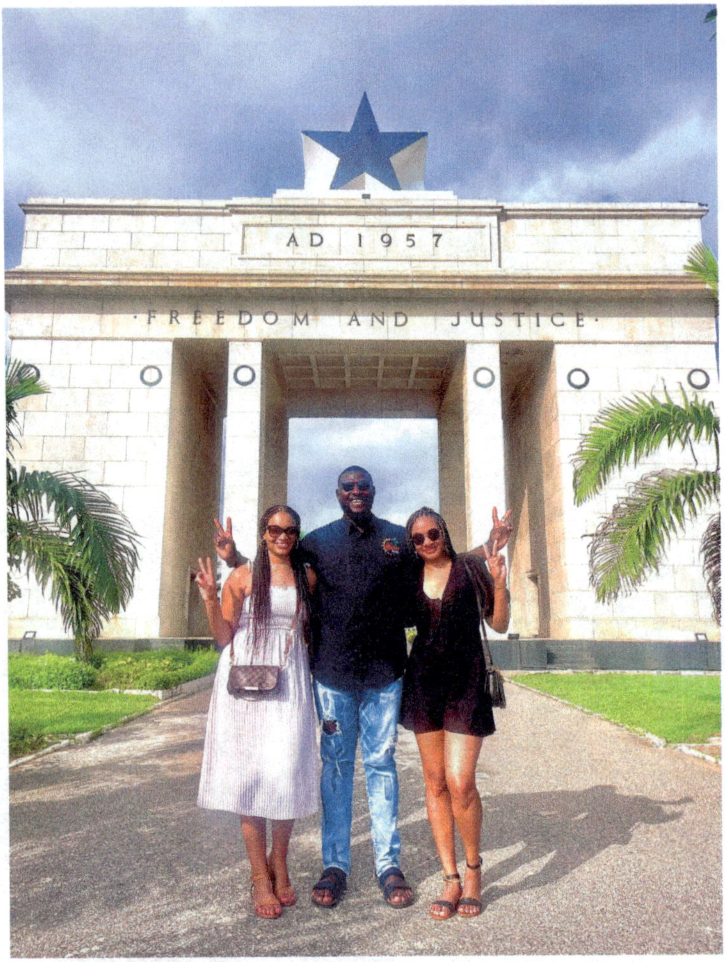
AD 1957
·FREEDOM AND JUSTICE·

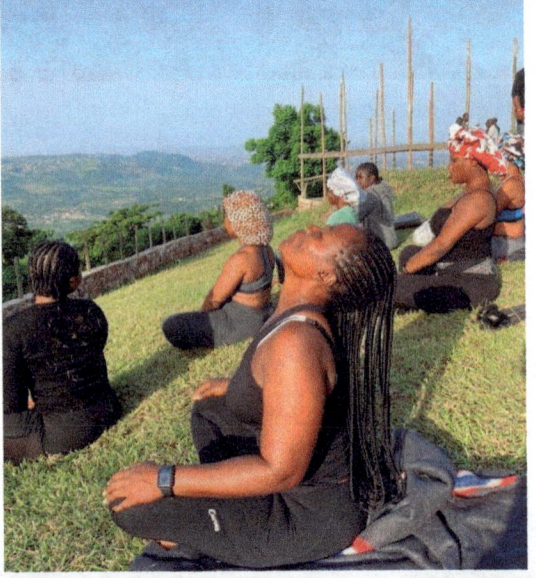

Uncovering Ghana's Hidden Gems with Abusua Travels

Ghana is a country that offers a unique and authentic travel experience. From the vibrant cities to the serene beaches, there is so much to explore and discover. As you plan your visit, there is no better way to experience the best of Ghana than by partnering with Abusua Travels.

At Abusua Travels, we have years of experience in providing tailored travel solutions for both individuals and groups. Our mission is to help you discover the real Ghana, from its rich culture and heritage to its natural beauty and wildlife. We are passionate about creating memorable experiences for our clients, and we are committed to making your visit to Ghana unforgettable.

Our tours are designed to give you an insider's perspective of Ghana. We take you to the must-see destinations such as Cape Coast Castle, Mole National Park, Wli Waterfalls, and many more. But we also show you the hidden gems that are often overlooked by other travel providers. We take you to the off-the-beaten-path locations, where you can experience the true essence of Ghana's culture and way of life.

Abusua Travels offers a variety of tour packages to suit every budget and interest. Whether you are looking for a cultural, adventure, or wildlife experience, we have the perfect package for you. Our tours are designed to be flexible and customizable, allowing you to make the most of your time in Ghana. We take care of all the details, so you can relax and enjoy your trip.

Our team of experienced travel consultants and guides are committed to providing exceptional service to all our clients. From the moment you arrive at the airport, we will take care of all your needs, including transportation, accommodation, and activities. Our guides are knowledgeable, friendly, and passionate about sharing their love of Ghana with you.

Abusua Travels offers a range of additional services to enhance your travel experience. We can assist with visa applications, flight bookings, and travel insurance, ensuring that you have a hassle-free trip.

At Abusua Travels, we are committed to making your visit to Ghana a memorable one. Our aim is to create lasting memories and friendships that will stay with you long after your trip has ended. We are dedicated to providing exceptional service, tailored to your needs and interests.

So why not join us on a journey of discovery, and experience the best of Ghana with Abusua Travels. We look forward to welcoming you to Ghana and helping you discover the treasures of this beautiful country.

Book Your Trip Today!

07 –10 APRIL, 2023

For a group Trip of 5 people

20% OFF

KWAHU EASTER

WEEKEND BREAK

ONLY GHS 4,500/PAX

- 2 Night / 3 Days
- 1/2 Star Hotel
- Breakfast / Dinner,
- Transportation
- Tours, fun activities
- Nightlife

MORE CONTACT INFO:
0302551221 – 0266206006
info@abusuatravels.com
www.abusuatravels.com

OFFICE
GD-107-2466 25 Boundary Rd. - East Legon

BOOK NOW | PAY LATER

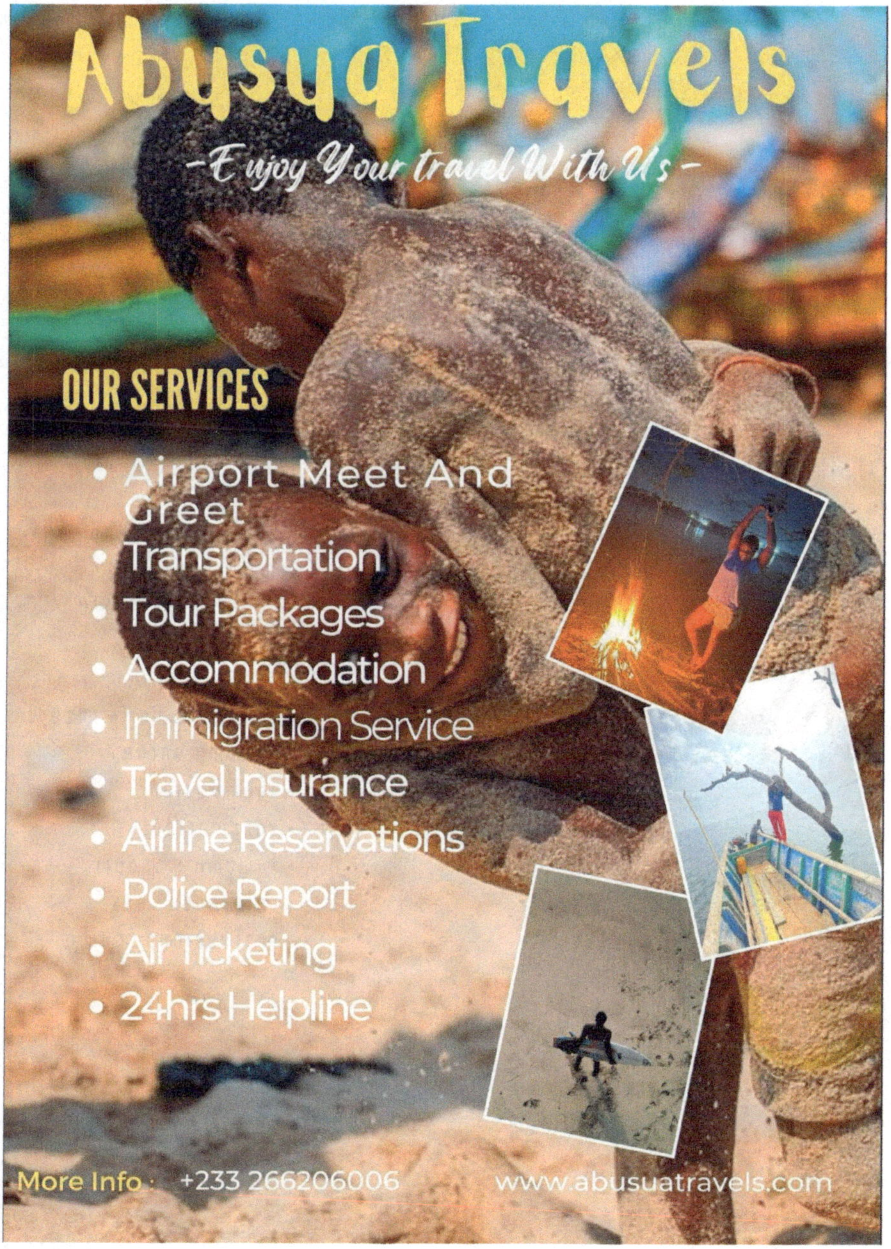
Abusua Travels
-Enjoy Your travel With Us-
OUR SERVICES
• Airport Meet And Greet
• Transportation
• Tour Packages
• Accommodation
• Immigration Service
• Travel Insurance
• Airline Reservations
• Police Report
• Air Ticketing
• 24hrs Helpline
More Info : +233 266206006
www.abusuatravels.com

EXPLORE
Shai hills & Akosombo

$185
PER PERSON

Package Inclusive

- Transportation
- Buffet | Water | Snacks
- SHAI HILLS GAME RESERVE
- AKWAMU GORGE
- ADOMI BRIDGE
- BOAT CURISE
- AKWAMU MUSEUM
- ENTRANCES FEES
- PROFESSIONAL GUIDE

Abusua Travels

BOOK NOW

📞 0266206006
✉ info@abusuatravels.com

QUAD BIKING
TOUR

$150 *per person*

Package Inclusive

Transportation
Breakfast & lunch
Bottles of water snacks
All tour charges
Quad bike
Asenema waterfall
Swimming
Professional guide

Abusua Travels

BOOK NOW ›

ℹ **0266206006**
www.abusuatravels.com

Made in the USA
Monee, IL
09 November 2023

46043042R00072